THE FUTURE OF American health care was never less certain than in the days before June 25, 2015. The U.S. Supreme Court had yet to issue a ruling in *King v. Burwell*, a potentially fatal challenge to the Patient Protection and Affordable Care Act, President Barack Obama's signature health reform package.

At stake? The future of Obamacare's insurance exchanges. A judgment against the administration would have effectively dismantled these marketplaces – and the law with them. A verdict in the government's favor would have preserved the status quo and saved Obamacare.

*King v. Burwell* asked the high court to consider whether the Affordable Care Act allowed the Internal Revenue Service to provide tax credits subsidizing health coverage through the federal government's HealthCare.gov exchange. The law's text explicitly states that credits are available through "an Exchange established by the State."

The meaning of *State* was far from academic. Thirty-four states opted not to build their own exchanges – and left the task to the federal government.

If the court read *State* at face value, then millions of Americans shopping in the federally operated exchange would lose the subsidies that made their health insurance affordable. And if millions of customers left HealthCare.gov, the cost of insurance for those remaining would spiral upward. After all, only those who thought they'd have expensive medical bills would keep paying for coverage.

As that process repeated, Obamacare's exchanges would collapse. And so would the law.

So in those first few days of the summer of 2015, the nation waited to learn whether the Supreme Court would save Obamacare as it had three summers prior, in June 2012.

Here's how *King v. Burwell* ended up before the U.S. Supreme Court.

Four cases challenging the IRS's authority to distribute subsidies through the federal exchange were launched in different parts of the country.

A three-judge panel of the U.S. Court of Appeals for the D.C. Circuit ruled against the government in *Halbig v. Burwell* in July 2014. The U.S. District Court for the Eastern District of Oklahoma also ruled against the federal government in *Pruitt v. Burwell* in September 2014. The U.S. District Court for the Southern District of Indiana heard arguments in *Indiana v. IRS* in October 2014.

The U.S. Supreme Court chose to hear the fourth case. A Virginia man named David King, along with three others, hoped to avoid the requirement that he purchase health insurance. With subsidies, his insurance through HealthCare.gov would run $275 a month – an amount deemed "affordable" by the law and thus subjecting him to the law's individual mandate.

Without subsidies, he'd face monthly premiums of $648. The Affordable Care Act considered this latter sum "unaffordable," so King would be allowed to flout the individual mandate without penalty.

In other words, the subsidies would actually make King worse off by forcing him to spend $275 every month that he otherwise would not have spent.

King lost his case before the U.S. Court of Appeals for the Fourth Circuit and appealed to the Supremes.

*Burwell* in the case is Secretary of Health and Human Services Sylvia Mathews Burwell. Since her agency oversaw the implementation of the subsidy rule at the center of the case, she was named the defendant.

The plaintiff argued that he shouldn't have had to accept the federal government's largesse. Obamacare's text provided subsidies "through an Exchange established by the State." A straightforward reading would take

*State* to mean one of the 50. On top of that, the law specifically defines *State* as "each of the 50 States and the District of Columbia."

King was shopping for coverage in Virginia – one of the 34 states that never estab-

---

*For* King v. Burwell*'s dissenters, the majority's decision amounted to a willful misreading of the law.*

---

lished its own insurance exchange. But the Obama administration gave residents of the Old Dominion tax credits anyway. In doing so, the plaintiff argued, the IRS overstepped its authority and broke the law.

The administration, by contrast, posited that Obamacare's overall structure superseded one inartfully drafted phrase. Without subsidies, the exchanges would crumble. Congress couldn't possibly have meant for four words located deep within section 36b to blow up the entire law.

It followed, the government claimed, that any interpretation of the law prohibiting subsidies for federal-exchange customers was mistaken.

## *Saved by the Court*

The Supreme Court ended up ruling 6–3 against the plaintiffs. Chief Justice John Roberts wrote for the majority: "Congress passed the Affordable Care Act to improve health insurance markets, not to destroy them. If at all possible, we must interpret the Act in a way that is consistent with the former, and avoids the latter."

Tax credits would continue to flow through the federally operated exchanges. Approximately 5 million people would keep their subsidized coverage.

For the case's dissenters, the majority's decision amounted to a willful misreading of the law. Writing for the minority, Justice

Antonin Scalia expressed his concerns with characteristic bluntness: "Words no longer have meaning if an Exchange that is *not* established by a State is 'established by the State.'"

The majority's "somersaults of statutory interpretation," he continued, reveal the "discouraging truth that the Supreme Court of the United States favors some laws over others, and is prepared to do whatever it takes to uphold and assist its favorites."

"We should start calling the law SCOTUS-care," he concluded.

The Supreme Court had rescued Obamacare once again. Chief Justice Roberts had provided the same brand of "creative" legal reasoning he'd found to uphold the individual mandate back in 2012.

He may have believed that Congress did not intend to destroy America's health insurance market by passing Obamacare. But that's exactly what has happened.

\* \* \*

# THE IMPLICATIONS OF
# KING V. BURWELL

The *King* decision left Obamacare's systemic flaws intact. Those flaws have made coverage less affordable, diminished access to care for millions of Americans, limited networks of doctors and hospitals for those in the exchanges, and stymied economic growth.

Things will only get worse in the months and years to come – if Obamacare is not repealed and replaced.

## *Not-So-Affordable Care*

The price of coverage has skyrocketed since the Affordable Care Act (ACA) took effect.

Consider the rise in deductibles – the amount a consumer must pay before an insurance policy kicks in. In 2006, prior to Obamacare, the average individual plan deductible was $584, according to the Kaiser Family Foundation (KFF). By 2015, post-ACA, it had more than doubled – to $1,318.

For many Americans, these costs are too much to bear. Another KFF study found that 24 percent of non-elderly, non-poor families with private coverage don't have enough in liquid assets to cover the $1,200 to $2,400 deductible for a midrange insurance plan. Only two-thirds of that group have enough for a higher deductible.

The growth in deductibles doesn't just sap household finances. It also puts patients' health at risk. Two in five adults with deductibles totaling at least 5 percent of their income reported avoiding or putting off necessary medical care, according to the Commonwealth Fund.

Deductibles are only part of the problem. Insurance premiums have also risen at an alarming rate since the ACA took effect. According to a study of cities in 45 states by Health Pocket, a consumer health research tool, premiums for midlevel "silver" exchange plans will increase by 14 percent in 2016. For more generous "gold" plans, premiums will jump an average of 16 percent.

# *The* King *decision left Obamacare's systemic flaws intact.*

Average premiums for employer-based family coverage reached $17,545 in 2015, up from $16,834 in 2014.

Since 2008, when President Obama promised that his vision for health reform would "reduc[e] premiums by as much as $2,500 per family," premiums for the average family have surged by $4,865.

Unfortunately, the price of insurance will only increase. Among the reasons? A spate of Obamacare-fueled mergers among insurance companies that will make the market less competitive.

The ACA regulates everything from how much insurers can charge to what benefits they must cover. The law's medical-loss-ratio rules, for instance, require insurers in the individual and small-group markets to spend no less than 80 percent of premium revenue on medical claims. Administration and overhead can consume no more than 20 percent. In the large-group market, insurers must devote 85 percent or more of premiums to claims – and 15 percent or less to overhead.

These regulations have driven up insurers' expenses. So they've been looking for ways to cut costs. Merging with one another can provide short-term savings on overhead.

The nation's third-largest insurer, Aetna Inc., is teaming up with fourth-largest Humana Inc. Second-place Anthem Inc. is swallowing Cigna Corp., the fifth-largest insurer. The resulting company would be the country's largest insurer.

The Senate Judiciary Committee's Subcommittee on Antitrust, Competition Policy, and Consumer Rights held a hearing on the mergers on Sept. 22, 2015. If the federal Department of Justice ultimately approves these deals, insurance behemoths may soon dominate the market. Without serious competition, they'll have little problem hiking rates.

The upward march of premiums is bad news for not just consumers but for taxpayers too. Obamacare subsidizes the purchase of insurance for millions in the exchanges – 8.3 million as of June 30, 2015. Those subsidies depend, in part, on the price of the so-called benchmark silver exchange plan. If the price of that plan jumps, so too does the government's share of the cost.

Subsidies are available on a sliding scale to those who make between 138 percent and 400 percent of the federal poverty level. If premiums rise more quickly than wages – as they have historically – then the taxpayers' tab for subsidies will rise even further.

### Patient Access Denied

The ACA hasn't just proved unaffordable. It's also failing to improve access to care.

Consider those who purchase coverage on one of the ACA's insurance exchanges. For the most part, exchange plans offer limited provider networks. According to a study from the Robert Wood Johnson Foundation, 41 percent of exchange plans include less than one-quarter of nearby physicians in their networks. Many cover less than 10 percent of an area's doctors.

Compare that with the policies sold outside the ACA marketplaces. Avalere Health, a consultancy, found that exchange-plan networks included 34 percent fewer provider options than their nonexchange counterparts. Exchange customers have 42 percent fewer choices for oncology and heart specialists than the average person covered by a commercial plan.

These narrow networks have made it even harder for patients to find doctors. According to the Association of American Medical Colleges, there's currently a shortage of more than 20,000 physicians. That shortfall is projected to reach more than 91,000 by 2020.

The combination of physician shortages and limited provider networks has forced many Americans to endure lengthy waits before seeing a physician. A 2014 survey of physicians in 15 cities found that the average wait time for a new patient in five medical specialties was more than 18 days. Those seeking an appointment with a family physician in Boston waited an average of 66 days.

Patients who gained coverage through Obamacare's expansion of Medicaid – the joint federal-state health care program for low-income Americans who earn less than 133 percent of the federal poverty line – have found it even more difficult to get care. Through May 2015, more than 71 million Americans were enrolled in the program – 22 percent more than before the ACA went into effect.

Obamacare expanded Medicaid in part to try to keep low-income, uninsured Americans from seeking care in high-cost emergency rooms. The law's supporters reasoned that Medicaid enrollees would visit the doctor's office – a less costly environment for delivering care.

But doctors have long been reluctant to see Medicaid beneficiaries because of the program's inadequate reimbursement rates. A 2012 *Health Affairs* study found that nearly one-third of physicians refused to treat Medicaid patients. In 2014, the Department of Health and Human Services found that more than half of providers weren't able to offer appointments to Medicaid enrollees.

So the Medicaid expansion has done little to stop people from heading to emergency rooms. In fact, ERS are as crowded as ever. In a March 2015 survey of more than 2,000 emergency-room doctors nationwide, roughly three-quarters reported an increase in ER visits since January 2014.

Perhaps that shouldn't be surprising. A 2014 report conducted by MIT and Harvard researchers discovered that adult Medicaid beneficiaries use emergency rooms 40 percent more frequently than the uninsured.

But the rise in ER visits is only one way that Obamacare is putting undue strain on our nation's finances and our economy.

Health care spending accounts for more than 17 percent of America's gross domestic product, or nearly $3 trillion. By 2024, national health expenditures are projected to reach $5.4 trillion – almost 20 percent of the economy.

Consider the law's effects on employers. Beginning in 2015, Obamacare's employer mandate required firms with 100 or more employees to provide insurance to their workers. If they refused or failed to provide coverage that was deemed affordable or sufficiently comprehensive, they faced fines of $2,000 per worker, minus the first 30, or $3,000 per worker who received subsidies in the exchanges – whichever is less. Businesses with 50 to 99 workers must heed these rules starting in January 2016.

This employer mandate, in combination with the rapid growth in insurance premiums, is placing enormous financial strain on companies.

Some firms are trying to avoid the mandate by making full-time employees part-timers. *Investor's Business Daily* has tallied more than 450 private companies and government agencies that have cut hours. More than 200 colleges have done the same.

The Obamacare-fueled switch to part-time work is exacerbating our economy's struggle to create full-time jobs. Even though the recession officially ended six years ago, there are still more than 6 million people working part-time today who want full-time jobs. That's on top of the 8 million people who are unemployed.

Money will get tighter for employers in 2018, when the law's "Cadillac" tax kicks in. This provision will place a 40 percent excise tax on the cost of coverage in excess of $10,200 for individuals and $27,500 for families. That includes not just premiums but also contributions into tax-advantaged accounts, like health savings accounts and flexible spending accounts.

According to the National Business Group on Health, almost half of large employers will face the tax in its first year. By 2026, 94 percent of firms will be subject to it.

Making matters worse, the Cadillac tax doesn't account for medical inflation. The thresholds only grow at the rate of overall inflation plus 1 percent. That's problematic because in the past four years, employer premiums have surged an average of 5.2 percent a year – more than double the rate of general inflation.

All told, Obamacare is expected to cost large companies $151 billion to $186 billion through 2023, according to the American Health Policy Institute.

The law's impact on small and medium-size businesses has been especially pronounced. The American Action Forum estimates that Obamacare is squeezing $22.6 billion annually out of businesses with 20 to 99 employees.

According to an analysis by former Con-

> *The price of coverage has skyrocketed since the Affordable Care Act took effect. Two in five adults with deductibles totaling at least 5 percent of their income reported avoiding or putting off necessary medical care.*

gressional Budget Office Director Douglas Holtz-Eakin, workers at businesses with 50 to 99 employees are seeing annual wages drop by an average of $935 a year, thanks to the ACA. Yearly wages for those employed at companies with 20 to 49 workers are falling by more than $827, on average.

Then there are the job losses resulting from Obamacare's various taxes and regulations. In 2014, the Congressional Budget Office

(CBO) estimated that the ACA would cause 2 million job losses in 2017. By 2024, the CBO projected that the number would reach 2.5 million.

Seven in 10 small businesses report that Obamacare has made it harder for them to hire. Forty-one percent told Gallup they'd postponed hiring in response to the Affordable Care Act.

This disastrous economic fallout could lead to even more disastrous reforms to our health care system.

### *The Road to Socialized Medicine*

President Obama has never denied his sympathies for a single-payer health care system. "I happen to be a proponent of a single-payer universal health care program," he said in 2003, while running for U.S. Senate. He reiterated his support during the 2008 presidential campaign, saying, "If I were designing a system from scratch, I would probably go ahead with a single-payer system."

Political opposition in Congress has made his dreams of single-payer infeasible. But Obamacare's ongoing failure may lead to the very single-payer system he's always wanted.

How might such a scenario play out? To start, the federal government may take over the few state exchanges that still exist.

Oregon and Hawaii have already shuttered their exchanges for the federal HealthCare.gov marketplace. Nevada, meanwhile, has let the federal government handle its enrollment duties.

Only 13 states and the District of Columbia operate their own online marketplaces. And they aren't faring well.

Take the Covered California exchange. Despite receiving $1.1 billion in federal money, the exchange has faced severe technological problems. Things are so bad that Covered California's executive director, Peter Lee, admitted that the "long-term sustainability of the organization" remains an open question.

Taxpayers have put more than $189 million

> *The American Action Forum estimates that Obamacare is squeezing $22.6 billion annually out of businesses with 20 to 99 employees.*

into Minnesota's exchange. It managed to sign up about 60,000 people last year. It had hoped to enroll 100,000. Vermont's exchange will need $51 million a year to provide insurance to fewer than 32,000 enrollees – or $1,613 per enrollee in overhead. Washington State's exchange faces a deficit of $4.5 million.

As Kaiser Family Foundation senior vice president Larry Levitt recently explained, "Now that the law's in place, and the Supreme Court has said that subsidies are available in all states, there's really much less imperative for states to be running these things."

In other words, *King* unwittingly set the stage for single-payer. The billions of dollars in taxpayer money spent constructing state-based exchanges will have been wasted. Any pretense of state independence will be gone.

The president's push to further expand Medicaid's rolls represents yet another step toward socialized medicine. States have long struggled to finance the program, which is collectively their second-highest expenditure.

Ohio's Medicaid expansion was $1.5 billion over budget in its first 18 months. Kentucky's expansion is expected to cost roughly $1.8 billion more than expected in 2014 and 2015. Illinois's Medicaid program was $800 million in the red in 2014.

Federal funding for Obamacare's Medicaid expansion will decline starting in 2017, leaving the states to pick up an even greater share of the tab. Cash-strapped states may push the feds to take over Medicaid entirely.

Once Medicaid – and the related Children's Health Insurance Program – are fully federalized, it's only a matter of time before they're folded into Medicare, the costliest federal health program of them all.

At that point, Washington will be the chief provider of coverage for the elderly, the disabled, children, veterans, and low-income Americans. The only outliers will be those insured on the private market.

Obamacare has already driven the price of insurance for these "outliers" skyward. And it has pushed insurers to consolidate, which could increase costs further.

The exploding price of coverage will boost public support for the government to "do something." That something could be a full-scale takeover of the health care system. After all, the government already accounts for 43 percent of all health spending. Why not just cut out the middleman?

Federal officials will then have their best opportunity yet to swallow what's left of the private insurance market – and put in place the socialized system President Obama has pined for.

By leaving Obamacare unscathed, the Supreme Court has unwittingly put America on the road to a single-payer system. The only question is whether President Obama's replacement will turn the country off that path.

## A Replacement Plan for Obamacare

To do so, the next president must do more than commit to repealing Obamacare. He or she will need to enter the Oval Office with a plan for replacing it.

The goal of that plan should be simple – to allow market forces to expand consumers' choices and improve quality while reducing costs, just as they do in the rest of the economy.

The federal government has meddled in the health care market more than in just about any other. It has distorted prices and costs with inefficient tax policies, open-ended entitlement programs, costly mandates, and government-enforced limits on competition. Obamacare has only made things worse.

A replacement for Obamacare must address these decades-old faults. The solution to our nation's health care problems is not more government – it's less.

Here's my proposal for repealing and replacing Obamacare.

1. *Create a level playing field for health insurance*

The approximately 150 million Americans who get their health coverage through work enjoy the benefit tax-free, while those who purchase policies on their own must use post-tax dollars. This unequal treatment is a legacy of the 1940s, when the National War Labor Board ruled that federal wage and price controls didn't apply to health benefits. That decision allowed employers to skirt restrictions on what they could pay their workers by providing more-generous benefits.

Consequently, securing coverage through

work can save an employee thousands of dollars a year in taxes.

This decades-old inequity is the reason our employer-based system of first-dollar coverage exists. But it limits consumer choice and the ability to seek new employment opportunities, particularly for those with pre-existing conditions. If a person loses a job, he or she must purchase coverage with after-tax dollars. The system also insulates consumers from the cost of their care – and thus encourages people to overconsume.

## A. Refundable Tax Credits

To minimize these distortions, the best course of action is to extend refundable tax credits, which vary according to age, to any individual or family who does not get coverage through work.

Those credits should be set at the following levels: $1,200 for those ages 18 to 35; $2,100 for those between 35 and 50; $3,000 for those over 50; and $900 per child.

Representative Tom Price, R-Ga., the chairman of the House Budget Committee and an orthopedic surgeon, has proposed credits of those amounts in his Empowering Patients First Act, which he introduced in the House in 2013 and in 2015. Presidential hopefuls Senator Marco Rubio, R-Fla., and former Governor Jeb Bush, R-Fla., have similarly come out in favor of refundable tax credits, though they haven't specified how much those credits should be.

The federal government should distribute the credits directly to individuals instead of giving them to insurance companies, as Obamacare does with its subsi-

---

*The solution to our nation's health care problems is not more government — it's less.*

---

dies. That way, if individuals purchase insurance that costs less than the value of their credit, they could deposit the difference into a tax-advantaged health savings account, which allows people to set aside money tax-free for health expenses and roll it over from year to year.

The 2017 Project, a conservative reform group, has calculated that refundable credits of these amounts would be enough to cover most of the cost of individual insurance plans that were available prior to Obamacare.

Making the credit independent of income serves two purposes. First, it's simple. There's no need for a consumer to guess what he'll end up earning, reconcile matters at tax time, or hire a professional tax preparer to figure out where he fits into a complicated phaseout schedule.

Second, it's fair. Such a tax credit would benefit low-, middle-, and high-income Americans equally. And it wouldn't penalize low- and middle-income people for getting raises by reducing their subsidies, as Obamacare does.

For these two reasons, a uniform age-based credit is superior to some other ideas for using the tax code to subsidize the purchase of health insurance.

For instance, some lawmakers – including Louisiana Governor Bobby Jindal and the leaders of the House Republican Study Committee – have called for a uniform standard tax deduction. People could essentially deduct the amount they spend on health insurance from their taxable income, up to a certain cap, regardless of whether they obtained health insurance through work or on their own.

But a standard deduction for insurance would be of little use to those who pay little, if any, federal tax. With a refundable credit, everyone within a given age group would get the same amount, regardless of their tax situation.

Other health reformers have called for

income-based tax credits. A plan developed by Senator Richard Burr, R-N.C.; Senator Orrin Hatch, R-Utah; and Representative Fred Upton, R-Mich., would extend credits to those with incomes below 300 percent of the poverty line.

But income-based credits like those amount to little more than Obamacare Lite. Indeed, Democratic presidential candidate Hillary Clinton has proposed progressive refundable tax credits of up to $2,500 for individuals and $5,000 for families. Even worse, Clinton would fund those credits by extracting billions of dollars from pharmaceutical companies, which will only drive up drug prices for consumers.

*B. Cap the Tax Break for Employer Benefits*
The tax exclusion on employer-sponsored health insurance also needs to be capped. It's presently one of the biggest "tax expenditures" in the budget, valued at

$206 billion a year. Much of that benefit goes to wealthier workers, who tend to have more-generous health insurance.

Obamacare's Cadillac tax tries to limit this exemption but does so in a ham-fisted way. The tax applies to all expensive employer-based plans, whether they cover low-, middle-, or high-income employees. So a low-income earner would effectively face a new 40 percent excise tax on the value of any benefits that exceed the thresholds established by Obamacare.

Most of Obamacare's critics agree with the intent of the Cadillac tax – that is, to limit how much we're willing to subsidize insurance through the tax code. The present unlimited tax subsidy for health insurance encourages people to purchase expensive insurance – and thus drives up overall health spending.

A better approach than the Cadillac tax is to cap the tax exemption at $8,000 for individuals and $20,000 for family plans –

and then raise that ceiling each year by the rate of inflation plus 1 percent.

Capping the exclusion would cause low- or middle-income workers to pay taxes on the excess value at their normal income tax rate, which could be as low as 10 or 15 percent. Higher-income workers would pay higher penalties for exceeding the cap, as they're in higher tax brackets.

My proposed caps are the same as Price's. Burr, Hatch, and Upton have argued for more-generous ones — at $12,000 for individuals and $30,000 for family plans. Jeb Bush's plan would cap the exclusion at the same levels. But with the average cost of employer health benefits in 2015 at $6,251 for an individual and $17,545 for a family, the Burr-Hatch-Upton and Bush limits are needlessly excessive.

Ultimately, it would be preferable to eliminate employer-based coverage and switch to a system in which individuals secure health insurance on their own.

Governor Jindal argues for doing so right away, by ending the tax exemption for employer plans altogether.

Decoupling insurance from employment will take time. Senator Rubio argues that 10 years should be enough. He'd equalize the employer tax exclusion and his refundable tax credits within a decade to "prevent large-scale disruptions and reform one of the most significant distortions in our tax system."

## 2. *Unleash Competition in the Insurance Market*

State and federal mandates, along with restrictions on who can offer insurance and where, have sharply limited competition in the insurance market and thus raised prices for consumers.

Any free-market reform plan must remove these impediments. Small businesses should be allowed to band together to increase their buying power. Associations with large, nationwide memberships should be free to offer health benefits to members.

Expanding access to group insurance would also help people with pre-existing conditions find affordable coverage.

Letting consumers buy coverage across state lines is also crucial. As it stands, consumers can find themselves trapped in states with dozens of costly benefit mandates requiring coverage for such things as chiropractic care and in vitro fertilization. These mandates, collectively, can raise the cost of a basic insurance policy by 30 percent to 50 percent.

Permitting people to shop in other states for insurance plans that meet their individual needs would put pressure on states to roll back mandates or risk losing business – and the tax revenue that comes along with it – to states with less burdensome regulatory systems. It stands to reason that increased competition among insurers and regulators – as well as the increased availability of policies with fewer cost-inflating mandates – would lead to lower prices for consumers.

In fact, prior to the passage of Obamacare, economist Stephen Parente and three co-authors calculated that interstate insurance sales would allow 12 million previously uninsured people to buy insurance, simply by making policies more affordable.

Opponents of interstate insurance sales on the left claim that the move will prompt a "race to the bottom," whereby state regulators gut consumer-protection regulations and insurers compete to sell the skimpiest policies possible.

But there's no evidence that the folks who are currently forced to shop in states with few regulations – like Idaho – are any worse off than those in heavily regulated states, like New York. In fact, the data suggest that states with fewer mandates simply have lower premiums.

Meanwhile, some conservative critics of interstate insurance sales claim the move won't accomplish much. As Merrill Matthews, a resident scholar at the Institute for Policy Innovation, told the *New York Times*, "Just because a good affordable policy is available in another state doesn't mean that I would be able to get the network of physicians and the good prices that are available in that other state."

---

*Medicare and Medicaid comprise 20 percent and 15 percent of national health spending, respectively.*

---

That may be true. But it's no justification for keeping interstate insurance sales illegal.

Most Republicans support opening up the health insurance marketplace – even Donald Trump, who has previously expressed sympathy for other countries' single-payer health care systems.

Of course, Trump also said in an interview

with Scott Pelley on CBS's *60 Minutes* that "the government's gonna pay for" his "terrific" replacement plan for Obamacare, so it's anyone's guess whether he actually favors expanding competition in the insurance marketplace – or just says he does.

### 3. *Put Consumers in the Driver's Seat*

In 1965, 48 percent of the nation's health costs were paid out of pocket. About 11 percent are today. Third-party payers – insurance, Medicare, Medicaid, and other government programs – pick up the rest.

The result has been an explosion in medical spending and inflation, an avalanche of paperwork, costly administrative infrastructure, and opaque pricing.

Health savings accounts can help reverse this trend by returning control over health care spending to consumers. People in HSA plans spend 21 percent less on health care in their first year, according to a RAND Corporation study. HSA costs are running one-quarter less than those for conventional insurance plans.

HSAs have become popular since they first hit the market in 2004. There are about 14.5 million of them, and the collective assets in those accounts amount to more than $28 billion.

Unfortunately, the federal government restricts who is eligible, how much they can put into an HSA, and what the money within them can buy. Those rules need to be relaxed. To start, individuals should be able to open HSAs if they have lower-deductible health plans – rather than just plans with deductibles set at arbitrarily high levels.

The legal limits on HSA contributions should match those for IRAs. In 2015, those limits were $5,500 per person – and $6,500 for those 50 or older. That would be up from the 2015 and 2016 individual HSA contribution limit of $3,350.

To further encourage the adoption of

HSAs, a replacement for Obamacare should include a one-time, refundable $1,000 tax credit for anyone who opens one.

The system of refundable tax credits can further bolster HSAs – by allowing people to deposit any unused portion of their credit into an HSA.

These are the basics of Representative Price's approach to HSAs. The House Republican Study Committee would set the contribution limits at similar levels, equal to the annual limit on out-of-pocket expenses under an HSA-qualified plan. Jeb Bush would do the same. In 2016, those limits will be $6,550 for individuals and $13,100 for families.

Senator Rubio and the Burr-Hatch-Upton troika also support expanding HSAs, but thus far they've been light on the details.

### 4. *Protect Those With Pre-Existing Conditions*

One of Obamacare's most popular provisions is its guarantee of affordable coverage to anyone at any time, regardless of pre-existing conditions.

Obamacare attempts to make good on this guarantee by mandating that insurers sell to all comers and controlling the prices they can charge – the "guaranteed issue" and "community rating" rules. To discourage people from gaming the system, Obamacare orders everyone to get coverage or pay a fine – the hated individual mandate.

But the fines – the greater of $325 per person or 2 percent of income in 2015, and $695 or 2.5 percent of income from 2016 onward – are so low as to be toothless. The entire scheme effectively encourages folks to wait until they get sick to purchase insurance.

The pre-existing-condition problem can be solved without destroying the insurance market and making coverage expensive for everyone. Reformers must simply require insurers to cover anyone who has had continuous coverage for the prior year without taking health status or history into consideration – and do so without increasing premiums to unaffordable levels.

We already know this approach works, since it currently exists in some fashion in the employer market.

Unlike Obamacare, this reform would actually encourage people, particularly "young invincibles," to buy insurance. Indeed, about half the 10.5 million uninsured in 2015 were between the ages of 18 and 34.

Under this replacement plan, once they have and keep coverage, they're protected from rate hikes or denials should they later need to switch plans.

Most of the alternatives to Obamacare – whether full-fledged legislative proposals or rough outlines from presidential candidates – provide similar protections for those who maintain continuous coverage.

### 5. Restore High-Risk Pools for the Truly Needy

One of Obamacare's few good ideas was to establish high-risk pools in every state. Such pools can guarantee affordable coverage for those with pre-existing conditions who cannot find it in the conventional market. And they help keep rates lower in the conventional market by removing the highest-cost people from the standard insurance pool.

Unfortunately, Obamacare's high-risk pools dried up once the exchanges opened. The funds dedicated to them were exhausted well before the exchanges opened. Those enrolled in the high-risk pools had to transfer to the exchanges to get coverage. And as a result, insurance costs have since skyrocketed.

Properly established and funded, high-risk pools can work and provide a safety net for those who are unable to buy or afford insurance in the conventional market.

If and when the United States gets a properly functioning health insurance market, where coverage is owned by consumers, then the high-risk pools could be abandoned, as the insurance risk pool would be large enough to affordably cover people of all health statuses.

Price would provide $1 billion a year for high-risk pools, with an eye on closing them in 2018. The House Republican Study Committee would furnish $25 billion over 10 years. Rubio, Bush, and Burr-Hatch-Upton also support rebooting state-based high-risk pools.

Jindal would give states $100 billion over 10 years to cover patients who can't find affordable coverage because of pre-existing conditions, with fewer strings attached.

The 2017 Project calls for $7.5 billion a year in federal funding for high-risk pools. This is probably the most realistic estimate of what it would cost to seed a network of high-risk pools that can guarantee affordable coverage to those who can't get it in the standard marketplace – without walloping taxpayers.

### 6. *Rein in Liability Abuses*

Today's medical-liability system encourages overtreatment by providers who practice defensive medicine to protect themselves against potential lawsuits. The risk of such lawsuits boosts the cost of malpractice insurance – a cost that is passed on to consumers and health insurers. Estimates of the cost of defensive medicine range from tens of billions to hundreds of billions of dollars a year.

A replacement for Obamacare must push the states – which have jurisdiction over medical liability – to create courts staffed by experts to evaluate plaintiffs' claims and establish legal standards that protect doctors who follow best medical practices.

The Price plan would do both, while the Republican Study Committee proposal would do just the latter.

The trio of Burr, Hatch, and Upton would go further by instituting federal caps on non-economic damages and attorneys' fees in medical-liability suits. This brand of reform is better left to the states.

### 7. *End Costly, Open-Ended Entitlements*

Medicare and Medicaid comprise 20 percent and 15 percent of national health spending, respectively. As the population ages, those shares will only grow.

Taxpayers cannot afford these open-ended entitlements anymore. Medicare spending is projected to double by 2024, to more than $1.2 trillion.

Medicaid is in similarly dire straits. Spending in the program will grow from $475 billion in 2014 to $900 billion by 2024, according to the Centers for Medicare and Medicaid Services. The program already consumes 24 percent of state budgets.

Any credible health reform plan must tackle these crises head-on – and do so in ways that maximize consumer choice, improve quality, and save money.

The solution for Medicaid is simple – replace the current funding formula with a series of block grants to states. Then allow states to administer their Medicaid programs in ways that meet the needs of their low-income populations.

Burr, Hatch, and Upton champion this approach. Instead of open-ended Medicaid spending, they're calling for "capped allot-ment," whereby federal funding for the pro-gram would be adjusted based on demographic and population changes and would grow over time at inflation plus 1 percent. In exchange for these fixed payments, states would have "significant latitude" in how they run their programs.

Jeb Bush also favors reforming Medicaid via capped allotments. Senator Rubio, mean-while, wants to cap Medicaid funding on a per-person basis.

Wisconsin Governor Scott Walker offered an interesting approach to Medicaid reform before dropping out of the presidential race. He proposed splitting the program into three parts.

The first, which he called Medical Assis-tance for Needy Families, would include capped allotments to states. States would be free to determine eligibility, coverage, and cost sharing.

The second piece would continue as an open-ended matching program covering acute care services for disabled people and low-income seniors. The third piece would alter Medicaid's long-term-care insurance program, which would be transformed into a capped allotment.

Those ideas belong in the reform conversation, even with Walker no longer in the race for president.

As for Medicare, the solution is equally straightforward. For starters, raise the eligibility age to 67. Seniors are living nine years longer, on average, than they did in 1965, when the program was created. Life expectancy will rise to 84 by 2050.

Then let seniors shop for insurance, just like they shop for everything else. Means-tested "premium support," "defined contributions," or "vouchers" could help them pay for their policies. Lawmakers should also allow Medicare beneficiaries to contribute to HSAs, which the program currently prohibits.

Seniors would be free to buy whatever plan suits them, supplementing their vouchers with their own cash. Insurers would have to compete for seniors' business. Such competition would rein in Medicare's runaway costs.

Rubio and Jindal have floated these Medicare reform ideas on the presidential campaign trail. And House Ways and Means Chairman Paul Ryan, R-Wis., has made premium support the centerpiece of his vision for Medicare reform.

## What's at Stake

Following his victory in *King v. Burwell*, President Obama declared, "The Affordable Care Act is here to stay."

But that may not be the case. If opponents of the law take Congress and the presidency, then the process for repealing and replacing Obamacare can begin in earnest on Jan. 20, 2017 – the day Obama leaves the White House.

Repealing Obamacare would have a positive effect on the economy. The Congressional Budget Office projects that repeal would increase GDP by 0.7 percent from 2021 to 2025. That translates to more than $117 billion in new economic activity.

Repeal would also remove more than a trillion dollars' worth of spending commitments from the federal budget over the next decade. And it would finally allow policymakers to deconstruct the third-party, employer-based system that has accelerated the growth of health costs by offering "first-dollar coverage"

---

*Repealing Obamacare would have a positive effect on the economy.*

---

for employees for decades.

There are several viable market-based plans for replacing Obamacare. All would rely on market forces to empower doctors and patients to take direct control of health care and drive down costs in the process.

The time for action will be soon. The longer our leaders wait, the more the law will become entrenched in American society and difficult to unwind. Government intrusion into the health care marketplace will increase until Americans are the unwitting victims of a government-run Medicare-for-all system.

Indeed, President Obama's would-be heirs are already advocating such a future. Democratic presidential candidate Hillary Clinton rolled out her plan for Obamacare 2.0 in late September 2015. In addition to her proposed tax credits, she'd require insurance companies to cover three visits to the doctor per year outside any deductible. Clinton also proposes federalizing insurance-rate review for states that do not adequately modify or block premium hikes.

She has called for new government price controls on prescription drugs too. Clinton would give Medicare the power to negotiate prices directly with drug manufacturers. Given the size of the Medicare market, the government doesn't negotiate prices – it dictates them.

Clinton's plan would also cap monthly prescription-drug spending at $250 for those with chronic conditions – and allow Americans to import price-controlled medications from other countries.

Such moves would essentially freeze medical progress – and lead to shortages and rationing of critical medicines, as is common in countries with single-payer systems that directly control drug prices.

Senator Bernie Sanders, D-Vt., meanwhile, has promised to implement a full-fledged single-payer health care system if elected president. The cost? A cool $15 trillion over 10 years.

The American people must stop the march toward single-payer. Repealing and replacing Obamacare will set the groundwork for a freer, happier, and more prosperous nation.

© 2015 by Sally C. Pipes

First American edition published in 2015 by Encounter Books, an activity of Encounter for Culture and Education, Inc., a nonprofit, tax exempt corporation.
Encounter Books website address: www.encounterbooks.com

Manufactured in the United States and printed on acid-free paper. The paper used in this publication meets the minimum requirements of ANSI/NISO z39.48–1992 (R 1997) (*Permanence of Paper*).

FIRST AMERICAN EDITION

LIBRARY OF CONGRESS
CATALOGING-IN-PUBLICATION DATA
IS AVAILABLE

10 9 8 7 6 5 4 3 2 1